Self care for the fourth trimester

Dr. Krystal Monique

BFF Publishing House is a Limited Liability Corporation dedicated wholly to the appreciation and publication of books for children and adults for the advancement of diversification in literature.

For more information on publishing contact:

Antionette Mutcherson, MBA at
bff@bffpublishinghouse.com
Website: bffpublishinghouse.com
Published in the United States by
BFF Publishing House
Atlanta, Georgia First Edition, 2022

Welcome

Congratulations, Mama! You did it. You literally grew a whole human, sis, and brought life into this world. You're a superhero!

Note to reader

As a first-time mother of fraternal twin girls, it hit me that the woman who existed pre-motherhood is no longer here. My life is divided into B.C. and A.D.—"before children" and "after daughters." I'm a new person and I embrace it. I am reborn and giving myself grace unlike ever before. As a new mother, it's important that I am the best version of myself, always adding to my cup so I have enough to pour from.

Dear Mama,

You're doing great! Now, take five minutes each evening to reflect on the day, your environment, and your goals. Take a minute to rest, reflect, restore, and prepare to set intentions and reflections for a full life.

How to use this journal

Some days, self-care looks like spending a little extra time in the bathroom to apply my facial toner, serum, and moisturizer. Other days, it looks like simply taking a long, hot shower. This journal is designed for the new mother, the new woman, to remind yourself of how important you are to you and how important it is to take your time.

This book contains quotes on self-love, body image, self-awareness, and growth as you journey into the fourth trimester—a.k.a. motherhood.

It is designed to be an outlet for new moms who are undergoing the stress, the uncertainty, the fear, the anxiety, and the fatigue of this unfamiliar experience. It's okay to be tired.

"The moment a child is born, the mother is also born. She never existed before. The woman existed, but the mother, never. A mother is something absolutely new."

— Bhagwan Shree Rajneesh

Date: _____

I am practicing self-care today by

_____

_____

I feel amazing about myself when

_____

_____

I am a good mama because

_____

_____

The best part of my day was

_____

_____

What feels like a struggle at the moment?

_____

_____

"Once I became a mother, I didn't know who I was anymore—until I realized this was a new version of myself that I had never met before. I had to learn her."

— Dr. Krystal Monique"

Date: _____

I am practicing self-care today by

_____

_____

I feel amazing about myself when

_____

_____

I am a good mama because

_____

_____

The best part of my day was

_____

_____

What feels like a struggle at the moment?

_____

_____

""Mama, you are ENOUGH!"

— Shaquana Robotham"

Date: _____

I am practicing self-care today by

_____

_____

I feel amazing about myself when

_____

_____

I am a good mama because

_____

_____

The best part of my day was

_____

_____

What feels like a struggle at the moment?

_____

_____

Keep taking control and time for yourself, until you're you again.

Date: _____

I am practicing self-care today by

_____

_____

I feel amazing about myself when

_____

_____

I am a good mama because

_____

_____

The best part of my day was

_____

_____

What feels like a struggle at the moment?

_____

_____

"There's no way to be a perfect mother and a million ways to be a good one."

— Jill Churchill

Date: _____

I am practicing self-care today by

_____

_____

I feel amazing about myself when

_____

_____

I am a good mama because

_____

_____

The best part of my day was

_____

_____

What feels like a struggle at the moment?

_____

_____

PARENTHOOD IS FUCKING HARD. I thought it would be easy. Everyone fucking does it. How hard can it be? Oh, it's HARD, BUT IT'S PHENOMENAL."

— Adele

Date: _____

I am practicing self-care today by

_____

_____

I feel amazing about myself when

_____

_____

I am a good mama because

_____

_____

The best part of my day was

_____

_____

What feels like a struggle at the moment?

_____

_____

"Dear Self: Action also requires rest. Give yourself permission to do both."

— Alex Elle

Date: _____

I am practicing self-care today by

_____

_____

I feel amazing about myself when

_____

_____

I am a good mama because

_____

_____

The best part of my day was

_____

_____

What feels like a struggle at the moment?

_____

_____

"Being a mother is learning about strengths you didn't know you had and dealing with fears you never knew existed."

— Linda Wooten

Date: _____

I am practicing self-care today by

_____

_____

I feel amazing about myself when

_____

_____

I am a good mama because

_____

_____

The best part of my day was

_____

_____

What feels like a struggle at the moment?

_____

_____

"Giving grace to yourself is never more important than when you became a mother."

— Whitney Meade

Date: _____

I am practicing self-care today by

_____

_____

I feel amazing about myself when

_____

_____

I am a good mama because

_____

_____

The best part of my day was

_____

_____

What feels like a struggle at the moment?

_____

_____

"Motherhood is a miracle and your body does some miraculous things during pregnancy. Give yourself grace during the postpartum period."

— Giovannii Salkey

Date: _____

I am practicing self-care today by

_____

_____

I feel amazing about myself when

_____

_____

I am a good mama because

_____

_____

The best part of my day was

_____

_____

What feels like a struggle at the moment?

_____

_____

"I can be grateful that I am a mom, while finding it hard at the same time."

— Shaquana Robotham

Date: _____

I am practicing self-care today by

_____

_____

I feel amazing about myself when

_____

_____

I am a good mama because

_____

_____

The best part of my day was

_____

_____

What feels like a struggle at the moment?

_____

_____

Becoming a mother allows me to embrace my whole, incredible self.

Date: _____

I am practicing self-care today by

_____

_____

I feel amazing about myself when

_____

_____

I am a good mama because

_____

_____

The best part of my day was

_____

_____

What feels like a struggle at the moment?

_____

_____

"We may not be perfect mothers, but we are the perfect mothers for our children."

— Unknown

Date: _____

I am practicing self-care today by

_____

_____

I feel amazing about myself when

_____

_____

I am a good mama because

_____

_____

The best part of my day was

_____

_____

What feels like a struggle at the moment?

_____

_____

"Life is tough, but so are you."

— Stephanie Bennett Henry

Date: _____

I am practicing self-care today by

_____

_____

I feel amazing about myself when

_____

_____

I am a good mama because

_____

_____

The best part of my day was

_____

_____

What feels like a struggle at the moment?

_____

_____

"This is your experience. Shape it, mold it, however you see fit."

—Dr. Krystal Monique

.

Date: _____

I am practicing self-care today by

_____

_____

I feel amazing about myself when

_____

_____

I am a good mama because

_____

_____

The best part of my day was

_____

_____

What feels like a struggle at the moment?

_____

_____

A mother's love endures through all."

— Washington Irving

Date: _____

I am practicing self-care today by

_____

_____

I feel amazing about myself when

_____

_____

I am a good mama because

_____

_____

The best part of my day was

_____

_____

What feels like a struggle at the moment?

_____

_____

"The days are long, but the years are short."

— Gretchen Rubin

Date: _____

I am practicing self-care today by

_____

_____

I feel amazing about myself when

_____

_____

I am a good mama because

_____

_____

The best part of my day was

_____

_____

What feels like a struggle at the moment?

_____

_____

"Almost everything will work again if you unplug it for a few minutes, including you."

— Ann Lamont

Date: _____

I am practicing self-care today by

_____

_____

I feel amazing about myself when

_____

_____

I am a good mama because

_____

_____

The best part of my day was

_____

_____

What feels like a struggle at the moment?

_____

_____

Don't forget to be patient with your process.

Date: _____

I am practicing self-care today by

_____

_____

I feel amazing about myself when

_____

_____

I am a good mama because

_____

_____

The best part of my day was

_____

_____

What feels like a struggle at the moment?

_____

_____

"Keep taking time for yourself until you're you again."

— Lalah Delia

Date: _____

I am practicing self-care today by

_____

_____

I feel amazing about myself when

_____

_____

I am a good mama because

_____

_____

The best part of my day was

_____

_____

What feels like a struggle at the moment?

_____

_____

"Self-care is giving the world the best of you, instead of what's left of you."

— Katie Reed

Date: _____

I am practicing self-care today by

_____

_____

I feel amazing about myself when

_____

_____

I am a good mama because

_____

_____

The best part of my day was

_____

_____

What feels like a struggle at the moment?

_____

_____

"You owe yourself the love that you so freely give to other people."

Date: _____

I am practicing self-care today by

_____

_____

I feel amazing about myself when

_____

_____

I am a good mama because

_____

_____

The best part of my day was

_____

_____

What feels like a struggle at the moment?

_____

_____

Remember to prioritize yourself. Don't forget who you are.

Date: _____

I am practicing self-care today by

_____

_____

I feel amazing about myself when

_____

_____

I am a good mama because

_____

_____

The best part of my day was

_____

_____

What feels like a struggle at the moment?

_____

_____

"Don't forget you're human. It's okay to have a meltdown. Just don't unpack and live there. Refocus on where you're headed."

— Unknown

Date: _____

I am practicing self-care today by

_____

_____

I feel amazing about myself when

_____

_____

I am a good mama because

_____

_____

The best part of my day was

_____

_____

What feels like a struggle at the moment?

_____

_____

"To your children, you are home. Whatever that looks like to you doesn't compare to how they view you."

— Dr. Krystal Monique

Date: _____

I am practicing self-care today by

_____

_____

I feel amazing about myself when

_____

_____

I am a good mama because

_____

_____

The best part of my day was

_____

_____

What feels like a struggle at the moment?

_____

_____

"Dear Mama, you are appreciated."

— Tupac Shakur

Date: _____

I am practicing self-care today by

_____

_____

I feel amazing about myself when

_____

_____

I am a good mama because

_____

_____

The best part of my day was

_____

_____

What feels like a struggle at the moment?

_____

_____

"Birth takes a woman's deepest fears about herself and shows her that she is stronger than them."

— Unknown

Date: _____

I am practicing self-care today by

_____

_____

I feel amazing about myself when

_____

_____

I am a good mama because

_____

_____

The best part of my day was

_____

_____

What feels like a struggle at the moment?

_____

_____

"Making the decision to have a child is momentous. It is to decide forever to have your heart go walking around outside your body."

— Elizabeth Stone

Date: _____

I am practicing self-care today by

_____

_____

I feel amazing about myself when

_____

_____

I am a good mama because

_____

_____

The best part of my day was

_____

_____

What feels like a struggle at the moment?

_____

_____

"Taking care of myself doesn't mean, 'Me first.' It means, 'Me, too.'"

— L.R. Knost

Date: _____

I am practicing self-care today by

_____

_____

I feel amazing about myself when

_____

_____

I am a good mama because

_____

_____

The best part of my day was

_____

_____

What feels like a struggle at the moment?

_____

_____

"Some days, you'll feel accomplished; most days, you won't. But every day, you gave your best."

— Dr. Krystal Monique

Date: _____

I am practicing self-care today by

_____

_____

I feel amazing about myself when

_____

_____

I am a good mama because

_____

_____

The best part of my day was

_____

_____

What feels like a struggle at the moment?

_____

_____

"Just because you become a mother, it doesn't mean you lose who you are."

— Beyoncé Knowles–Carter

Date: _____

I am practicing self-care today by

_____

_____

I feel amazing about myself when

_____

_____

I am a good mama because

_____

_____

The best part of my day was

_____

_____

What feels like a struggle at the moment?

_____

_____

My birth experience does not define my motherhood experience.

Date: _____

I am practicing self-care today by

_____

_____

I feel amazing about myself when

_____

_____

I am a good mama because

_____

_____

The best part of my day was

_____

_____

What feels like a struggle at the moment?

_____

_____

"I'm thankful to have a healthy baby."

— Jenell Solages

Date: _____

I am practicing self-care today by

_____

_____

I feel amazing about myself when

_____

_____

I am a good mama because

_____

_____

The best part of my day was

_____

_____

What feels like a struggle at the moment?

_____

_____

My unique body is beautiful. My body heals, nurtures, and provides.

Date: _____

I am practicing self-care today by

_____

_____

I feel amazing about myself when

_____

_____

I am a good mama because

_____

_____

The best part of my day was

_____

_____

What feels like a struggle at the moment?

_____

_____

My journey is special and should never be compared to another's.

Date: _____

I am practicing self-care today by

_____

_____

I feel amazing about myself when

_____

_____

I am a good mama because

_____

_____

The best part of my day was

_____

_____

What feels like a struggle at the moment?

_____

_____

"You can only pour into your children when your cup is full. Take the time to take care of you."

— Giovannii Salkey

Date: _____

I am practicing self-care today by

_____

_____

I feel amazing about myself when

_____

_____

I am a good mama because

_____

_____

The best part of my day was

_____

_____

What feels like a struggle at the moment?

_____

_____

Self-care is not a luxury, or a privilege. It's a responsibility.

Date: _____

I am practicing self-care today by

_____

_____

I feel amazing about myself when

_____

_____

I am a good mama because

_____

_____

The best part of my day was

_____

_____

What feels like a struggle at the moment?

_____

_____

I am perfect and complete just the way I am.

Date: _____

I am practicing self-care today by

_____

_____

I feel amazing about myself when

_____

_____

I am a good mama because

_____

_____

The best part of my day was

_____

_____

What feels like a struggle at the moment?

_____

_____

My life is what I make of it. I have all the power.

Date: _____

I am practicing self-care today by

_____

_____

I feel amazing about myself when

_____

_____

I am a good mama because

_____

_____

The best part of my day was

_____

_____

What feels like a struggle at the moment?

_____

_____

"There are hard days in motherhood, but looking at your baby sleeping reminds you why it's all worth it."

— Kara Ferwerda

Date: _____

I am practicing self-care today by

_____

_____

I feel amazing about myself when

_____

_____

I am a good mama because

_____

_____

The best part of my day was

_____

_____

What feels like a struggle at the moment?

_____

_____

My body is a vessel for my awesomeness.

Date: _____

I am practicing self-care today by

_____

_____

I feel amazing about myself when

_____

_____

I am a good mama because

_____

_____

The best part of my day was

_____

_____

What feels like a struggle at the moment?

_____

_____

Being grounded and whole makes me beautiful. I can get there just by being still, breathing, listening to my intuition, and doing what I can to be kind to myself and others.

Date: _____

I am practicing self-care today by

_____

_____

I feel amazing about myself when

_____

_____

I am a good mama because

_____

_____

The best part of my day was

_____

_____

What feels like a struggle at the moment?

_____

_____

"Even if I don't see how amazing I am, there is someone who does, and they call me Mama."

— Dr. Krystal Monique

Date: _____

I am practicing self-care today by

_____

_____

I feel amazing about myself when

_____

_____

I am a good mama because

_____

_____

The best part of my day was

_____

_____

What feels like a struggle at the moment?

_____

_____

I am loved and admired.

Date: _____

I am practicing self-care today by

_____

_____

I feel amazing about myself when

_____

_____

I am a good mama because

_____

_____

The best part of my day was

_____

_____

What feels like a struggle at the moment?

_____

_____

I use my energy to pay attention to myself, my inner wisdom, my virtues, my path, and my journey.

Date: _____

I am practicing self-care today by

_____

_____

I feel amazing about myself when

_____

_____

I am a good mama because

_____

_____

The best part of my day was

_____

_____

What feels like a struggle at the moment?

_____

_____

"Don't hold yourself to any of your previous standards. Set new ones."

— Dr. Krystal Monique

Date: _____

I am practicing self-care today by

_____

_____

I feel amazing about myself when

_____

_____

I am a good mama because

_____

_____

The best part of my day was

_____

_____

What feels like a struggle at the moment?

_____

_____

My well-being is the most important thing to me. I am responsible for taking care of me.

Date: _____

I am practicing self-care today by

_____

_____

I feel amazing about myself when

_____

_____

I am a good mama because

_____

_____

The best part of my day was

_____

_____

What feels like a struggle at the moment?

_____

_____

"To all mothers in every circumstance, including those who struggle, I say,
'Be peaceful. Believe in God and yourself. You are doing better than you think
you are.'"

— Jeffrey R. Holland

Date: _____

I am practicing self-care today by

_____

_____

I feel amazing about myself when

_____

_____

I am a good mama because

_____

_____

The best part of my day was

_____

_____

What feels like a struggle at the moment?

_____

_____

Hey, it's your journey! Own it!

Date: _____

I am practicing self-care today by

_____

_____

I feel amazing about myself when

_____

_____

I am a good mama because

_____

_____

The best part of my day was

_____

_____

What feels like a struggle at the moment?

_____

_____

"You're here on a mission and you're powerful. It's time to remember who you are."

— Lalah Delia

Date: _____

I am practicing self-care today by

_____

_____

I feel amazing about myself when

_____

_____

I am a good mama because

_____

_____

The best part of my day was

_____

_____

What feels like a struggle at the moment?

_____

_____

"To be a good parent, you need to take care of yourself so that you can have the physical and emotional energy to take care of your family."

— Michelle Obama

Date: _____

I am practicing self-care today by

_____

_____

I feel amazing about myself when

_____

_____

I am a good mama because

_____

_____

The best part of my day was

_____

_____

What feels like a struggle at the moment?

_____

_____

"Talk to yourself like you would to someone you love."

— Bréne Brown

Date: _____

I am practicing self-care today by

_____

_____

I feel amazing about myself when

_____

_____

I am a good mama because

_____

_____

The best part of my day was

_____

_____

What feels like a struggle at the moment?

_____

_____

New mamas are newborns, too. Be gentle.

Date: _____

I am practicing self-care today by

_____

_____

I feel amazing about myself when

_____

_____

I am a good mama because

_____

_____

The best part of my day was

_____

_____

What feels like a struggle at the moment?

_____

_____

"Good moms have homes that are clean enough to be healthy and messy enough to be happy."

— Unknown

Date: _____

I am practicing self-care today by

_____

_____

I feel amazing about myself when

_____

_____

I am a good mama because

_____

_____

The best part of my day was

_____

_____

What feels like a struggle at the moment?

_____

_____

"An empty tank will take you exactly nowhere. Take time to refuel."

— Unknown

Date: _____

I am practicing self-care today by

_____

_____

I feel amazing about myself when

_____

_____

I am a good mama because

_____

_____

The best part of my day was

_____

_____

What feels like a struggle at the moment?

_____

_____

"Now is not forever."

— Unknown

Date: _____

I am practicing self-care today by

_____

_____

I feel amazing about myself when

_____

_____

I am a good mama because

_____

_____

The best part of my day was

_____

_____

What feels like a struggle at the moment?

_____

_____

I love my body and I love myself.

Date: _____

I am practicing self-care today by

_____

_____

I feel amazing about myself when

_____

_____

I am a good mama because

_____

_____

The best part of my day was

_____

_____

What feels like a struggle at the moment?

_____

_____

"My body has changed. My life has changed. I am forever changing."

— Shaquana Robotham

Date: _____

I am practicing self-care today by

_____

_____

I feel amazing about myself when

_____

_____

I am a good mama because

_____

_____

The best part of my day was

_____

_____

What feels like a struggle at the moment?

_____

_____

"Meet today's problems with today's strength. Don't start tackling tomorrow's problems until tomorrow. You do not have tomorrow's strength yet. You simply have enough for today."

— Max Lucado

Date: _____

I am practicing self-care today by

_____

_____

I feel amazing about myself when

_____

_____

I am a good mama because

_____

_____

The best part of my day was

_____

_____

What feels like a struggle at the moment?

_____

_____

"I know you're tired. I know you're physically and emotionally drained. But you have to keep going."

— Unknown

Date: _____

I am practicing self-care today by

_____

_____

I feel amazing about myself when

_____

_____

I am a good mama because

_____

_____

The best part of my day was

_____

_____

What feels like a struggle at the moment?

_____

_____

"Life is what happens to you while you're busy making other plans."

— John Lennon

Date: _____

I am practicing self-care today by

_____

_____

I feel amazing about myself when

_____

_____

I am a good mama because

_____

_____

The best part of my day was

_____

_____

What feels like a struggle at the moment?

_____

_____

"You can't pour from an empty cup."

— Unknown

Date: _____

I am practicing self-care today by

_____

_____

I feel amazing about myself when

_____

_____

I am a good mama because

_____

_____

The best part of my day was

_____

_____

What feels like a struggle at the moment?

_____

_____

"Let's prove to ourselves that the judgment of others does not define us, that we are strong, brave, capable women who can do whatever the heck we set our minds to! Let us also remind each other when we forget."

— Julie Maida

Date: _____

I am practicing self-care today by

_____

_____

I feel amazing about myself when

_____

_____

I am a good mama because

_____

_____

The best part of my day was

_____

_____

What feels like a struggle at the moment?

_____

_____

"Parenting is hard. Especially when you're doing it right."

— Kristen Welch

Date: _____

I am practicing self-care today by

_____

_____

I feel amazing about myself when

_____

_____

I am a good mama because

_____

_____

The best part of my day was

_____

_____

What feels like a struggle at the moment?

_____

_____

"Don't let a bad day make you feel like you have a bad life."

— Unknown

Date: _____

I am practicing self-care today by

_____

_____

I feel amazing about myself when

_____

_____

I am a good mama because

_____

_____

The best part of my day was

_____

_____

What feels like a struggle at the moment?

_____

_____

"Start where you are. Use what you have. Do what you can."

— Arthur Ashe

Date: _____

I am practicing self-care today by

_____

_____

I feel amazing about myself when

_____

_____

I am a good mama because

_____

_____

The best part of my day was

_____

_____

What feels like a struggle at the moment?

_____

_____

"Being a mother is learning about strengths you didn't know you had, and dealing with fears you didn't know existed."

— Nishan Panwar

Date: _____

I am practicing self-care today by

_____

_____

I feel amazing about myself when

_____

_____

I am a good mama because

_____

_____

The best part of my day was

_____

_____

What feels like a struggle at the moment?

_____

_____

"The attitude you have as a parent is what your kids will learn from more than what you tell them. They don't remember what you try to teach them. They remember what you are."

— Jim Henson

Date: _____

I am practicing self-care today by

_____

_____

I feel amazing about myself when

_____

_____

I am a good mama because

_____

_____

The best part of my day was

_____

_____

What feels like a struggle at the moment?

_____

_____

"Behind every great child is a mom who's pretty sure she's screwing it all up."

— Unknown

Date: _____

I am practicing self-care today by

_____

_____

I feel amazing about myself when

_____

_____

I am a good mama because

_____

_____

The best part of my day was

_____

_____

What feels like a struggle at the moment?

_____

_____

"There will be so many times you feel like you failed. But in the eyes, ears, and mind of your child, you are a supermom."

— Stephanie Precourt

Date: _____

I am practicing self-care today by

_____

_____

I feel amazing about myself when

_____

_____

I am a good mama because

_____

_____

The best part of my day was

_____

_____

What feels like a struggle at the moment?

_____

_____

"I realized when you look at your mother, you are looking at the purest love you will ever know."

— Mitch Albom

Date: _____

I am practicing self-care today by

_____

_____

I feel amazing about myself when

_____

_____

I am a good mama because

_____

_____

The best part of my day was

_____

_____

What feels like a struggle at the moment?

_____

_____

"As a mother, my job is to take care of the possible and trust God with the impossible."

— Ruth Bell Graham.

Date: _____

I am practicing self-care today by

_____

_____

I feel amazing about myself when

_____

_____

I am a good mama because

_____

_____

The best part of my day was

_____

_____

What feels like a struggle at the moment?

_____

_____

"Be patient with yourself. The journey between practice and perfect is mistakes."

— Toloupe Dyewole

Date: _____

I am practicing self-care today by

_____

_____

I feel amazing about myself when

_____

_____

I am a good mama because

_____

_____

The best part of my day was

_____

_____

What feels like a struggle at the moment?

_____

_____

"The mind is everything. What you think, you become."

— Buddha

Date: _____

I am practicing self-care today by

_____

_____

I feel amazing about myself when

_____

_____

I am a good mama because

_____

_____

The best part of my day was

_____

_____

What feels like a struggle at the moment?

_____

_____

"Life is 10% what happens to you and 90% how you react to it."

— Charles Swindoll

Date: _____

I am practicing self-care today by

_____

_____

I feel amazing about myself when

_____

_____

I am a good mama because

_____

_____

The best part of my day was

_____

_____

What feels like a struggle at the moment?

_____

_____

"All mothers are working mothers."

— Unknown

Date: _____

I am practicing self-care today by

_____

_____

I feel amazing about myself when

_____

_____

I am a good mama because

_____

_____

The best part of my day was

_____

_____

What feels like a struggle at the moment?

_____

_____

"You should never replace your name with the word Mom because it's the first step to losing yourself. You have other things to offer the world."

— Magan Forrester

Date: _____

I am practicing self-care today by

_____

_____

I feel amazing about myself when

_____

_____

I am a good mama because

_____

_____

The best part of my day was

_____

_____

What feels like a struggle at the moment?

_____

_____

"Let today be the start of something new."

— Unknown

Date: _____

I am practicing self-care today by

_____

_____

I feel amazing about myself when

_____

_____

I am a good mama because

_____

_____

The best part of my day was

_____

_____

What feels like a struggle at the moment?

_____

_____

"Motherhood: All love begins and ends there.'"

— Robert Browning

Date: _____

I am practicing self-care today by

_____

_____

I feel amazing about myself when

_____

_____

I am a good mama because

_____

_____

The best part of my day was

_____

_____

What feels like a struggle at the moment?

_____

_____

"No one even mentioned it—in nine whole months, not one person said, 'You're about to meet someone entirely new. And it's not your baby; it's going to be you.'"

— Unknown

Date: _____

I am practicing self-care today by

_____

_____

I feel amazing about myself when

_____

_____

I am a good mama because

_____

_____

The best part of my day was

_____

_____

What feels like a struggle at the moment?

_____

_____

"Self-care teaches me that I can pour into myself just as much as I pour into others."

— Alex Elle

Date: _____

I am practicing self-care today by

_____

_____

I feel amazing about myself when

_____

_____

I am a good mama because

_____

_____

The best part of my day was

_____

_____

What feels like a struggle at the moment?

_____

_____

"Don't rush the process. It takes time returning to yourself."

— Lalah Delia

Date: _____

I am practicing self-care today by

_____

_____

I feel amazing about myself when

_____

_____

I am a good mama because

_____

_____

The best part of my day was

_____

_____

What feels like a struggle at the moment?

_____

_____

"One day, she is healing; the next day, she is breaking again. Both days, she is not giving up."

— Unknown

Date: _____

I am practicing self-care today by

_____

_____

I feel amazing about myself when

_____

_____

I am a good mama because

_____

_____

The best part of my day was

_____

_____

What feels like a struggle at the moment?

_____

_____

"You're going to get advice from a lot of people, and you can take bits and pieces, but you know innately what your child needs. You should trust that."

— Lucy Liu

Date: _____

I am practicing self-care today by

_____

_____

I feel amazing about myself when

_____

_____

I am a good mama because

_____

_____

The best part of my day was

_____

_____

What feels like a struggle at the moment?

_____

_____

"This is my perfect. It may not be somebody else's, but this is mine."

— Kerry Washington

Date: _____

I am practicing self-care today by

_____

_____

I feel amazing about myself when

_____

_____

I am a good mama because

_____

_____

The best part of my day was

_____

_____

What feels like a struggle at the moment?

_____

_____

"Get rid of the guilt. When you're at one place, don't feel bad that you're not at work. When you're at work, don't feel bad that you're not at home."

— Katie Couric

Date: _____

I am practicing self-care today by

_____

_____

I feel amazing about myself when

_____

_____

I am a good mama because

_____

_____

The best part of my day was

_____

_____

What feels like a struggle at the moment?

_____

_____

Accept what your body wants to be.

Date: _____

I am practicing self-care today by

_____

_____

I feel amazing about myself when

_____

_____

I am a good mama because

_____

_____

The best part of my day was

_____

_____

What feels like a struggle at the moment?

_____

_____

"Right now, my little FUPA and I feel like we are meant to be."

— Beyoncé Knowles-Carter

Date: _____

I am practicing self-care today by

_____

_____

I feel amazing about myself when

_____

_____

I am a good mama because

_____

_____

The best part of my day was

_____

_____

What feels like a struggle at the moment?

_____

_____

"My goal is to appreciate my body for what it has done."

— Sia Cooper

Date: _____

I am practicing self-care today by

_____

_____

I feel amazing about myself when

_____

_____

I am a good mama because

_____

_____

The best part of my day was

_____

_____

What feels like a struggle at the moment?

_____

_____

"I had a baby. I'm a superhero."

— Kelly Rowland

Date: _____

I am practicing self-care today by

_____

_____

I feel amazing about myself when

_____

_____

I am a good mama because

_____

_____

The best part of my day was

_____

_____

What feels like a struggle at the moment?

_____

_____

"You are worth the quiet moment. You are worth the deeper breaths and you are worth the time it takes to slow down, be still, and rest."

— Morgan Harper Nichols

Date: _____

I am practicing self-care today by

_____

_____

I feel amazing about myself when

_____

_____

I am a good mama because

_____

_____

The best part of my day was

_____

_____

What feels like a struggle at the moment?

_____

_____

"Take a pause to appreciate how far you've come."

— Lalah Delia

Date: _____

I am practicing self-care today by

_____

_____

I feel amazing about myself when

_____

_____

I am a good mama because

_____

_____

The best part of my day was

_____

_____

What feels like a struggle at the moment?

_____

_____

If we can't love and care for ourselves, how are we supposed to love & care for others?

Date: _____

I am practicing self-care today by

_____

_____

I feel amazing about myself when

_____

_____

I am a good mama because

_____

_____

The best part of my day was

_____

_____

What feels like a struggle at the moment?

_____

_____

"Today, I choose to appreciate myself for doing the necessary work to break generational curses."

— Maegan Henderson

Date: _____

I am practicing self-care today by

_____

_____

I feel amazing about myself when

_____

_____

I am a good mama because

_____

_____

The best part of my day was

_____

_____

What feels like a struggle at the moment?

_____

_____

I love myself the way I am.

Date: _____

I am practicing self-care today by

_____

_____

I feel amazing about myself when

_____

_____

I am a good mama because

_____

_____

The best part of my day was

_____

_____

What feels like a struggle at the moment?

_____

_____

"I don't know if I'm bouncing back. I'm slowly crawling back. You just have to be gentle and patient with yourself and just sort of, you know … slowly get back to your health."

— Reese Witherspoon

Date: _____

I am practicing self-care today by

_____

_____

I feel amazing about myself when

_____

_____

I am a good mama because

_____

_____

The best part of my day was

_____

_____

What feels like a struggle at the moment?

_____

_____

"Say goodbye to your inner critic, and take this pledge to be kinder to yourself."

— Oprah Winfrey

Date: _____

I am practicing self-care today by

_____

_____

I feel amazing about myself when

_____

_____

I am a good mama because

_____

_____

The best part of my day was

_____

_____

What feels like a struggle at the moment?

_____

_____

"Beauty is about being comfortable in your skin. It's about knowing and respecting who you are."

— Ellen Degeneres

Date: _____

I am practicing self-care today by

_____

_____

I feel amazing about myself when

_____

_____

I am a good mama because

_____

_____

The best part of my day was

_____

_____

What feels like a struggle at the moment?

_____

_____

"It always seems impossible until it's done."

— Nelson Mandela

Date: _____

I am practicing self-care today by

_____

_____

I feel amazing about myself when

_____

_____

I am a good mama because

_____

_____

The best part of my day was

_____

_____

What feels like a struggle at the moment?

_____

_____

Find rest for your soul.

Date: _____

I am practicing self-care today by

_____

_____

I feel amazing about myself when

_____

_____

I am a good mama because

_____

_____

The best part of my day was

_____

_____

What feels like a struggle at the moment?

_____

_____

"Protect your energy at all costs."

— Dr. Krystal Monique

Date: _____

I am practicing self-care today by

_____

_____

I feel amazing about myself when

_____

_____

I am a good mama because

_____

_____

The best part of my day was

_____

_____

What feels like a struggle at the moment?

_____

_____

"Never doubt your intuition. It doesn't have to make sense to anyone else; only you."

— Magan Forrester

Date: _____

I am practicing self-care today by

_____

_____

I feel amazing about myself when

_____

_____

I am a good mama because

_____

_____

The best part of my day was

_____

_____

What feels like a struggle at the moment?

_____

_____

"Savor every moment, take a million pictures and videos, don't be too hard on yourself, and work on your patience."

— Giovannii Salkey

Date: _____

I am practicing self-care today by

_____

_____

I feel amazing about myself when

_____

_____

I am a good mama because

_____

_____

The best part of my day was

_____

_____

What feels like a struggle at the moment?

_____

_____

"There's no snapping back. This is a whole new me."

— Nurse Mo

Date: _____

I am practicing self-care today by

_____

_____

I feel amazing about myself when

_____

_____

I am a good mama because

_____

_____

The best part of my day was

_____

_____

What feels like a struggle at the moment?

_____

_____

"Take time to enjoy being a first time mother... and know there is not right or wrong. This is a learning experience for everyone involved, even if they have their own kids, because every child is different.

— Jenell Solages

Date: _____

I am practicing self-care today by

_____

_____

I feel amazing about myself when

_____

_____

I am a good mama because

_____

_____

The best part of my day was

_____

_____

What feels like a struggle at the moment?

_____

_____

"As a mom, we can't stay who we once were. Our children are evolving, and so should we."

— Shaquana Robotham

Date: _____

I am practicing self-care today by

_____

_____

I feel amazing about myself when

_____

_____

I am a good mama because

_____

_____

The best part of my day was

_____

_____

What feels like a struggle at the moment?

_____

_____

"Taking time for myself has become a nonnegotiable part of my spiritual practice."

— Lalah Delia

Date: _____

I am practicing self-care today by

_____

_____

I feel amazing about myself when

_____

_____

I am a good mama because

_____

_____

The best part of my day was

_____

_____

What feels like a struggle at the moment?

_____

_____

Remove the guilt and allow yourself to just be.

Date: _____

I am practicing self-care today by

_____

_____

I feel amazing about myself when

_____

_____

I am a good mama because

_____

_____

The best part of my day was

_____

_____

What feels like a struggle at the moment?

_____

_____

A mom expressing exhaustion doesn't correlate to her love for motherhood.

Date: _____

I am practicing self-care today by

_____

_____

I feel amazing about myself when

_____

_____

I am a good mama because

_____

_____

The best part of my day was

_____

_____

What feels like a struggle at the moment?

_____

_____

"At the end of the day, I just want to be a mama who defines her own motherhood journey, shows up for herself, and remembers to drink water."

— Maegan Henderson

Date: _____

I am practicing self-care today by

_____

_____

I feel amazing about myself when

_____

_____

I am a good mama because

_____

_____

The best part of my day was

_____

_____

What feels like a struggle at the moment?

_____

_____

Allow yourself to recharge.

Date: _____

I am practicing self-care today by

_____

_____

I feel amazing about myself when

_____

_____

I am a good mama because

_____

_____

The best part of my day was

_____

_____

What feels like a struggle at the moment?

_____

_____

A mother's body is beautiful!

Date: _____

I am practicing self-care today by

_____

_____

I feel amazing about myself when

_____

_____

I am a good mama because

_____

_____

The best part of my day was

_____

_____

What feels like a struggle at the moment?

_____

_____

"Give yourself the same love, patience, and grace you give those around you. She needs that from you, too."

— Meagan Henderson

Date: _____

I am practicing self-care today by

_____

_____

I feel amazing about myself when

_____

_____

I am a good mama because

_____

_____

The best part of my day was

_____

_____

What feels like a struggle at the moment?

_____

_____

"Don't ever stop believing in your personal transformation. It is happening even on the days you may not realize it or feel like it."

— Lalah Delia

Date: _____

I am practicing self-care today by

_____

_____

I feel amazing about myself when

_____

_____

I am a good mama because

_____

_____

The best part of my day was

_____

_____

What feels like a struggle at the moment?

_____

_____

When I show up for myself, I am able to show up for the people I love.

Date: _____

I am practicing self-care today by

_____

_____

I feel amazing about myself when

_____

_____

I am a good mama because

_____

_____

The best part of my day was

_____

_____

What feels like a struggle at the moment?

_____

_____

I can adapt to any change that life throws my way. I can find the good in any
situation. I surrender to the flow of life.

Date: _____

I am practicing self-care today by

_____

_____

I feel amazing about myself when

_____

_____

I am a good mama because

_____

_____

The best part of my day was

_____

_____

What feels like a struggle at the moment?

_____

_____

You may not be able to control your circumstances, but every day, you have control over how you view them.

Date: _____

I am practicing self-care today by

_____

_____

I feel amazing about myself when

_____

_____

I am a good mama because

_____

_____

The best part of my day was

_____

_____

What feels like a struggle at the moment?

_____

_____

Take time to nurture and recenter yourself.

Date: _____

I am practicing self-care today by

_____

_____

I feel amazing about myself when

_____

_____

I am a good mama because

_____

_____

The best part of my day was

_____

_____

What feels like a struggle at the moment?

_____

_____

Go within yourself and emit more grace and love.

Date: _____

I am practicing self-care today by

_____

_____

I feel amazing about myself when

_____

_____

I am a good mama because

_____

_____

The best part of my day was

_____

_____

What feels like a struggle at the moment?

_____

_____

Be kind and gentle with yourself.

Date: _____

I am practicing self-care today by

_____

_____

I feel amazing about myself when

_____

_____

I am a good mama because

_____

_____

The best part of my day was

_____

_____

What feels like a struggle at the moment?

_____

_____

Delegating, saying no, holding boundaries, and putting your needs before others' are all forms of self-care.

Date: _____

I am practicing self-care today by

_____

_____

I feel amazing about myself when

_____

_____

I am a good mama because

_____

_____

The best part of my day was

_____

_____

What feels like a struggle at the moment?

_____

_____

Do motherhood your way!

Date: _____

I am practicing self-care today by

_____

_____

I feel amazing about myself when

_____

_____

I am a good mama because

_____

_____

The best part of my day was

_____

_____

What feels like a struggle at the moment?

_____

_____

People may have feelings about your boundaries, parenting style, and personal choices, and that's fine.

Date: _____

I am practicing self-care today by

_____

_____

I feel amazing about myself when

_____

_____

I am a good mama because

_____

_____

The best part of my day was

_____

_____

What feels like a struggle at the moment?

_____

_____

When you prioritize yourself, everyone benefits.

Date: _____

I am practicing self-care today by

_____

_____

I feel amazing about myself when

_____

_____

I am a good mama because

_____

_____

The best part of my day was

_____

_____

What feels like a struggle at the moment?

_____

_____

The thing that screws us up the most is the picture in our head of how things are supposed to be.

Date: _____

I am practicing self-care today by

_____

_____

I feel amazing about myself when

_____

_____

I am a good mama because

_____

_____

The best part of my day was

_____

_____

What feels like a struggle at the moment?

_____

_____

When we let go of the need to be perfect and embrace our imperfections, we show our children that they can do the same.

Date: _____

I am practicing self-care today by

_____

_____

I feel amazing about myself when

_____

_____

I am a good mama because

_____

_____

The best part of my day was

_____

_____

What feels like a struggle at the moment?

_____

_____

Motherhood is relentless. It's normal to need a break. Take one.

Date: _____

I am practicing self-care today by

_____

_____

I feel amazing about myself when

_____

_____

I am a good mama because

_____

_____

The best part of my day was

_____

_____

What feels like a struggle at the moment?

_____

_____

Don't rush your postpartum healing.

Date: _____

I am practicing self-care today by

_____

_____

I feel amazing about myself when

_____

_____

I am a good mama because

_____

_____

The best part of my day was

_____

_____

What feels like a struggle at the moment?

_____

_____

"Having a baby is a psychological revolution that changes our relationship to nearly everything and everyone."

— Esther Perel

Date: _____

I am practicing self-care today by

_____

_____

I feel amazing about myself when

_____

_____

I am a good mama because

_____

_____

The best part of my day was

_____

_____

What feels like a struggle at the moment?

_____

_____

Motherhood is a constant state of transition.

Date: _____

I am practicing self-care today by

_____

_____

I feel amazing about myself when

_____

_____

I am a good mama because

_____

_____

The best part of my day was

_____

_____

What feels like a struggle at the moment?

_____

_____

"Being a mother is learning about strengths you didn't know you had...
and dealing with fears you didn't know existed."

— Linda Wooten

Date: _____

I am practicing self-care today by

_____

_____

I feel amazing about myself when

_____

_____

I am a good mama because

_____

_____

The best part of my day was

_____

_____

What feels like a struggle at the moment?

_____

_____

A good mom has bad days and good days and normal days and overwhelming days and perfect days and trying days and supermom days and "just being a mom" days and a whole lot of love and real and crazy motherhood days.

Date: _____

I am practicing self-care today by

_____

_____

I feel amazing about myself when

_____

_____

I am a good mama because

_____

_____

The best part of my day was

_____

_____

What feels like a struggle at the moment?

_____

_____

I trust in my abilities to provide love, nourishment, and safety for my baby.

Date: _____

I am practicing self-care today by

_____

_____

I feel amazing about myself when

_____

_____

I am a good mama because

_____

_____

The best part of my day was

_____

_____

What feels like a struggle at the moment?

_____

_____

I feel more confident in my mothering style every day.

Date: _____

I am practicing self-care today by

_____

_____

I feel amazing about myself when

_____

_____

I am a good mama because

_____

_____

The best part of my day was

_____

_____

What feels like a struggle at the moment?

_____

_____

I am free to be the kind of mother I want to be.

Date: _____

I am practicing self-care today by

_____

_____

I feel amazing about myself when

_____

_____

I am a good mama because

_____

_____

The best part of my day was

_____

_____

What feels like a struggle at the moment?

_____

_____

As my baby grows, so does my confidence as a mother. I listen to my inner wisdom and feel my self-doubt fade away

Date: _____

I am practicing self-care today by

_____

_____

I feel amazing about myself when

_____

_____

I am a good mama because

_____

_____

The best part of my day was

_____

_____

What feels like a struggle at the moment?

_____

_____

I can't be the best mom to my baby if I am depleted. I tune into my body's messages, and I seek help when something doesn't feel right.

Date: _____

I am practicing self-care today by

_____

_____

I feel amazing about myself when

_____

_____

I am a good mama because

_____

_____

The best part of my day was

_____

_____

What feels like a struggle at the moment?

_____

_____

I am exactly who my baby wants me to be.

Date: _____

I am practicing self-care today by

_____

_____

I feel amazing about myself when

_____

_____

I am a good mama because

_____

_____

The best part of my day was

_____

_____

What feels like a struggle at the moment?

_____

_____

Despite all of the challenges, sleepless nights, and frustrations, I feel gratitude for everything I have.

Date: _____

I am practicing self-care today by

_____

_____

I feel amazing about myself when

_____

_____

I am a good mama because

_____

_____

The best part of my day was

_____

_____

What feels like a struggle at the moment?

_____

_____

I embrace motherhood with joy and openness to possibility.

Date: _____

I am practicing self-care today by

_____

_____

I feel amazing about myself when

_____

_____

I am a good mama because

_____

_____

The best part of my day was

_____

_____

What feels like a struggle at the moment?

_____

_____

At this very moment, millions of other new moms are living through this phase alone with me. I am not alone.

Date: _____

I am practicing self-care today by

_____

_____

I feel amazing about myself when

_____

_____

I am a good mama because

_____

_____

The best part of my day was

_____

_____

What feels like a struggle at the moment?

_____

_____

"It's okay to take breaks. Take the time you need to feel your best."

— Shaquana Robotham

Date: _____

I am practicing self-care today by

_____

_____

I feel amazing about myself when

_____

_____

I am a good mama because

_____

_____

The best part of my day was

_____

_____

What feels like a struggle at the moment?

_____

_____

When I feel overwhelmed, I take a deep breath and center myself.

Date: _____

I am practicing self-care today by

_____

_____

I feel amazing about myself when

_____

_____

I am a good mama because

_____

_____

The best part of my day was

_____

_____

What feels like a struggle at the moment?

_____

_____

Motherhood is a journey, and I welcome each step.

Date: _____

I am practicing self-care today by

_____

_____

I feel amazing about myself when

_____

_____

I am a good mama because

_____

_____

The best part of my day was

_____

_____

What feels like a struggle at the moment?

_____

_____

With each inhale, I breathe in gratitude, positivity, joy, and love. With each exhale, I let go of expectations, disappointment, worry, and doubt.

Date: _____

I am practicing self-care today by

_____

_____

I feel amazing about myself when

_____

_____

I am a good mama because

_____

_____

The best part of my day was

_____

_____

What feels like a struggle at the moment?

_____

_____

I am a wonderful mom, and my baby loves me.

Date: _____

I am practicing self-care today by

_____

_____

I feel amazing about myself when

_____

_____

I am a good mama because

_____

_____

The best part of my day was

_____

_____

What feels like a struggle at the moment?

_____

_____

My baby is growing healthier and stronger every day, nourished by my love.

Date: _____

I am practicing self-care today by

_____

_____

I feel amazing about myself when

_____

_____

I am a good mama because

_____

_____

The best part of my day was

_____

_____

What feels like a struggle at the moment?

_____

_____

My body is amazing for birthing, nourishing, and protecting my baby.

Date: _____

I am practicing self-care today by

_____

_____

I feel amazing about myself when

_____

_____

I am a good mama because

_____

_____

The best part of my day was

_____

_____

What feels like a struggle at the moment?

_____

_____

I appreciate my body for what it is capable of. Every stretch mark, roll, and scar is beautiful for the love story it tells.

Date: _____

I am practicing self-care today by

_____

_____

I feel amazing about myself when

_____

_____

I am a good mama because

_____

_____

The best part of my day was

_____

_____

What feels like a struggle at the moment?

_____

_____

I cherish my body and treat her well.

Date: _____

I am practicing self-care today by

_____

_____

I feel amazing about myself when

_____

_____

I am a good mama because

_____

_____

The best part of my day was

_____

_____

What feels like a struggle at the moment?

_____

_____

I embrace the messiness of life as a new mom.

Date: _____

I am practicing self-care today by

_____

_____

I feel amazing about myself when

_____

_____

I am a good mama because

_____

_____

The best part of my day was

_____

_____

What feels like a struggle at the moment?

_____

_____

I let go of the need to control every aspect of my day.

Date: _____

I am practicing self-care today by

_____

_____

I feel amazing about myself when

_____

_____

I am a good mama because

_____

_____

The best part of my day was

_____

_____

What feels like a struggle at the moment?

_____

_____

I practice patience with myself because the best that I can do is good enough.

Date: _____

I am practicing self-care today by

_____

_____

I feel amazing about myself when

_____

_____

I am a good mama because

_____

_____

The best part of my day was

_____

_____

What feels like a struggle at the moment?

_____

_____

I am grateful for this season of my life.

Date: _____

I am practicing self-care today by

_____

_____

I feel amazing about myself when

_____

_____

I am a good mama because

_____

_____

The best part of my day was

_____

_____

What feels like a struggle at the moment?

_____

_____

I willingly ask for help so I can take a break.

Date: _____

I am practicing self-care today by

_____

_____

I feel amazing about myself when

_____

_____

I am a good mama because

_____

_____

The best part of my day was

_____

_____

What feels like a struggle at the moment?

_____

_____

Mothering is not meant to be done in isolation. My family, friends, and community are here to support me.

Date: _____

I am practicing self-care today by

_____

_____

I feel amazing about myself when

_____

_____

I am a good mama because

_____

_____

The best part of my day was

_____

_____

What feels like a struggle at the moment?

_____

_____

I will not let "mom guilt" hold me back from living a full and abundant life.

Date: _____

I am practicing self-care today by

_____

_____

I feel amazing about myself when

_____

_____

I am a good mama because

_____

_____

The best part of my day was

_____

_____

What feels like a struggle at the moment?

_____

_____

I am more than just a mom.

Date: _____

I am practicing self-care today by

_____

_____

I feel amazing about myself when

_____

_____

I am a good mama because

_____

_____

The best part of my day was

_____

_____

What feels like a struggle at the moment?

_____

_____

Motherhood is not a competition.

Date: _____

I am practicing self-care today by

_____

_____

I feel amazing about myself when

_____

_____

I am a good mama because

_____

_____

The best part of my day was

_____

_____

What feels like a struggle at the moment?

_____

_____

I let go of the desire to compare my journey to another mom's.

Date: _____

I am practicing self-care today by

_____

_____

I feel amazing about myself when

_____

_____

I am a good mama because

_____

_____

The best part of my day was

_____

_____

What feels like a struggle at the moment?

_____

_____

I embrace what makes my baby unique. I embrace what makes me unique.

Date: _____

I am practicing self-care today by

_____

_____

I feel amazing about myself when

_____

_____

I am a good mama because

_____

_____

The best part of my day was

_____

_____

What feels like a struggle at the moment?

_____

_____

My life is not perfect, but it's mine, and I choose to fill it with love, positivity, and laughter.

Date: _____

I am practicing self-care today by

_____

_____

I feel amazing about myself when

_____

_____

I am a good mama because

_____

_____

The best part of my day was

_____

_____

What feels like a struggle at the moment?

_____

_____

"You put something wonderful in the world that was not there before."

— Edwin Elliot

Date: _____

I am practicing self-care today by

_____

_____

I feel amazing about myself when

_____

_____

I am a good mama because

_____

_____

The best part of my day was

_____

_____

What feels like a struggle at the moment?

_____

_____

Love your extraordinary self!

Date: _____

I am practicing self-care today by

_____

_____

I feel amazing about myself when

_____

_____

I am a good mama because

_____

_____

The best part of my day was

_____

_____

What feels like a struggle at the moment?

_____

_____

"Children are never too young to be given an apology. It shows them that their feelings matter, too, and teaches the power of forgiveness."

— Magan Forrester

Date: _____

I am practicing self-care today by

_____

_____

I feel amazing about myself when

_____

_____

I am a good mama because

_____

_____

The best part of my day was

_____

_____

What feels like a struggle at the moment?

_____

_____

"Loving yourself is embracing your flaws—the bad, the ugly, the unspeakable, and the unbearable."

— Dr. Marquita Taylor

Date: _____

I am practicing self-care today by

_____

_____

I feel amazing about myself when

_____

_____

I am a good mama because

_____

_____

The best part of my day was

_____

_____

What feels like a struggle at the moment?

_____

_____

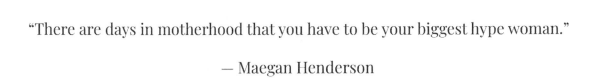

"There are days in motherhood that you have to be your biggest hype woman."

— Maegan Henderson

Date: _____

I am practicing self-care today by

_____

_____

I feel amazing about myself when

_____

_____

I am a good mama because

_____

_____

The best part of my day was

_____

_____

What feels like a struggle at the moment?

_____

_____

I can feel myself changing in all the right ways, and I love that for me.

Date: _____

I am practicing self-care today by

_____

_____

I feel amazing about myself when

_____

_____

I am a good mama because

_____

_____

The best part of my day was

_____

_____

What feels like a struggle at the moment?

_____

_____

Live your best, but it's even more important to GIVE your best, then take time to reset.

Date: _____

I am practicing self-care today by

_____

_____

I feel amazing about myself when

_____

_____

I am a good mama because

_____

_____

The best part of my day was

_____

_____

What feels like a struggle at the moment?

_____

_____

You will never be able to go back and change the beginning, but you can start where you are and change the ending.

Date: _____

I am practicing self-care today by

_____

_____

I feel amazing about myself when

_____

_____

I am a good mama because

_____

_____

The best part of my day was

_____

_____

What feels like a struggle at the moment?

_____

_____

"Be gentle with yourself and your body. You're doing the best you can."

— Shaquana Robotham

Date: _____

I am practicing self-care today by

_____

_____

I feel amazing about myself when

_____

_____

I am a good mama because

_____

_____

The best part of my day was

_____

_____

What feels like a struggle at the moment?

_____

_____

You are the exact mother your children need.

Date: _____

I am practicing self-care today by

_____

_____

I feel amazing about myself when

_____

_____

I am a good mama because

_____

_____

The best part of my day was

_____

_____

What feels like a struggle at the moment?

_____

_____

"Cherish all the moments. It goes by too fast."

— Jenell Solages

Date: _____

I am practicing self-care today by

_____

_____

I feel amazing about myself when

_____

_____

I am a good mama because

_____

_____

The best part of my day was

_____

_____

What feels like a struggle at the moment?

_____

_____

"You are not required to be a super mom or super woman to be loved fully by those who matter most. 'Super' is often a self-inflicted illusion or requirement from those who matter least."

— Mattie James

Date: _____

I am practicing self-care today by

_____

_____

I feel amazing about myself when

_____

_____

I am a good mama because

_____

_____

The best part of my day was

_____

_____

What feels like a struggle at the moment?

_____

_____

I assertively use my voice to express what I want and need and to say no when I'm uncomfortable.

Date: _____

I am practicing self-care today by

_____

_____

I feel amazing about myself when

_____

_____

I am a good mama because

_____

_____

The best part of my day was

_____

_____

What feels like a struggle at the moment?

_____

_____

I was divinely chosen and called to be the mother of this child, and I am good enough to care for them.

Date: _____

I am practicing self-care today by

_____

_____

I feel amazing about myself when

_____

_____

I am a good mama because

_____

_____

The best part of my day was

_____

_____

What feels like a struggle at the moment?

_____

_____

I welcome the challenge of motherhood with gratitude and a warm heart filled with love.

Date: _____

I am practicing self-care today by

_____

_____

I feel amazing about myself when

_____

_____

I am a good mama because

_____

_____

The best part of my day was

_____

_____

What feels like a struggle at the moment?

_____

_____

I always choose what's best for my baby and myself.

Date: _____

I am practicing self-care today by

_____

_____

I feel amazing about myself when

_____

_____

I am a good mama because

_____

_____

The best part of my day was

_____

_____

What feels like a struggle at the moment?

_____

_____

"Happy mommy ... happy baby ... happy life."

— Dr. Krystal Monique

Date: _____

I am practicing self-care today by

_____

_____

I feel amazing about myself when

_____

_____

I am a good mama because

_____

_____

The best part of my day was

_____

_____

What feels like a struggle at the moment?

_____

_____

It's not always easy, but it's so good. I'm very grateful for this family, this journey and this life.

- Jaclyn Warren

Date: _____

I am practicing self-care today by

_____

_____

I feel amazing about myself when

_____

_____

I am a good mama because

_____

_____

The best part of my day was

_____

_____

What feels like a struggle at the moment?

_____

_____

About The Author

Originally from Brooklyn NY, Dr. Krystal Monique studied Health and Physical education at Virginia State University where she obtained her Bachelors of Science, followed by her Masters of science in Occupational Therapy from Howard University. Subsequently, Dr. Krystal Monique went on to complete her Clinical Doctorate from Concordia University-Wisconsin. As an occupational therapist she has been privileged to combine her love for travel with her chosen career to complete several missionary trips and work with the underserved population. Her passion for helping others from a young age sparked a natural leadership string in her. She was always taught to speak her mind and advocate for herself and her peers.

Privy to the health disparities in predominantly women of color as a new mother Dr. Krystal Monique understood the challenges and stigmas motherhood may bring. Journaling has always been an outlet for her to unwind, center her thoughts and keep a self of calmness in an ever changing world. During her pregnancy she found many journals that she could relate to however during postpartum months she felt a void. Leading her to create her own prompts thus birthing *One Minute Mama.* Now 14 months into this motherhood journey and looking back at the various conversations she has had with family and friends she's learned that Grace and true centering are two key components to performing at her highest vibration.

From one Mama to another...take a minute for yourself.

Made in the USA
Middletown, DE
30 May 2023

31362003R00217